101 Things To Do With A Casserole

BY
STEPHANIE ASHCRAFT
AND JANET EYRING

Gibbs Smith, Publisher
Salt Lake City

First Edition
09 08 07   20 19 18 17 16 15 14 13 12 11 10 9 8 7 6 5

Text © 2005 Stephanie Ashcraft and Janet Eyring

Published by
Gibbs Smith, Publisher
P.O. Box 667
Layton, Utah 84041

Orders: 1.800.748.5439
www.gibbs-smith.com

Designed by Kurt Wahlner
Printed and bound in Korea

Library of Congress Cataloging-in-Publication Data

Ashcraft, Stephanie.
    101 things to do with a casserole / by Stephanie Ashcraft and Janet Eyring.—1st ed.
       p. cm.
    ISBN-13: 978-1-58685-823-0
    ISBN-10: 1-58685-823-8
    1. Casserole cookery. 2. One-dish meals. I. Title: One hundred and one things to do
with a casserole. II. Eyring, Janet. III. Title.
    TX693.A84 2005
    641.8'21—dc22
                        2005007470

To the good people in
Hibbard, Idaho, who we love so
dearly. Thank you for accepting us
into your community for the
year we lived there. And to my
dear teachers, especially Mrs.
Ruch, Mr. Robertson, and the late
Julia Pearson at Clinton Central
(Michigan Town, Indiana).
Thank you for teaching me to
always try my best. — S.A.

To my mother who had the
patience to teach an eight-year-old
girl how to cook. — J.E.

CONTENTS

Turkey

Pork

Beef

Family Favorites

HELPFUL HINTS

1. Always grease casserole pans or dishes with nonstick cooking spray for quick cleanup.

2. For the best results, use ceramic, glass, or stoneware baking dishes.

3. Bake casseroles on the middle oven rack. If possible, avoid the top and bottom racks.

4. The first time you try a recipe, check the casserole 5 minutes before its minimum cooking time. Each oven heats differently.

5. Many casseroles can be assembled the night before and stored in the refrigerator. Remove casserole from the refrigerator 20 minutes before baking.

6. Many casseroles can be assembled and frozen for use at a later date. Move the casserole from the freezer to the refrigerator 24 hours before baking. If casserole was frozen, it may take 10–15 minutes longer to bake. Bake until the temperature at the center of the casserole reaches 160 degrees F.

7. Avoid freezing casseroles that contain pasta or rice.

8. Low-fat, light, or low-sodium ingredients can be substituted in any recipe.

9. When using aluminum foil to cover casseroles, place the shiny side down toward the food. If the shiny side is facing up, it may reflect the heat and possibly increase cooking time.

10. Always cook the casserole in a preheated oven.

11. Condensed cream of chicken, cream of mushroom, and cream of celery soups can be used interchangeably.

12. Precook chicken in large quantities and freeze in 1-cup increments to save preparation time.

BREAKFAST

ASPARAGUS-ENGLISH MUFFIN BAKE

I pound	**fresh asparagus,** cut into I-inch pieces
5	**English muffins,** split and toasted
2 cups	**grated Colby Jack cheese,** divided
I $1/2$ cups	**diced fully cooked ham**
$1/2$ cup	**chopped red bell pepper**
8	**eggs,** beaten
2 cups	**milk**
I teaspoon	**salt**
I teaspoon	**dry mustard**
$1/2$ teaspoon	**black pepper**

In a 4-quart saucepan, boil asparagus pieces I minute. Drain and put in a large bowl of ice water to stop cooking process. Drain and pat asparagus dry with paper towels.

Place English muffin halves, cut side up, to form a crust in a greased 9 x 13-inch pan. Cut the muffins to fill the empty spaces in the pan as needed. Layer asparagus, half the cheese, ham, and bell pepper over muffins.

In a large bowl, whisk eggs, milk, salt, dry mustard, and pepper. Pour the egg mixture evenly over muffins. Cover and refrigerate 2 hours or overnight. Remove from refrigerator before preheating the oven to 375 degrees. Bake 40–45 minutes, or until set in the center. Immediately sprinkle remaining cheese over top and serve. Makes 6–8 servings.

BLUEBERRY FRENCH TOAST CASSEROLE

I loaf (20 ounces)	**bread,** cubed
I package (8 ounces)	**cream cheese,** cubed
I cup	**fresh** or **frozen blueberries**
12	**eggs,** beaten
2 cups	**milk**
I teaspoon	**vanilla**
$^1/_3$ cup	**maple syrup**
	powdered sugar

Place half the bread cubes in a greased 9 x 13-inch pan. Layer cream cheese cubes evenly over bread. Sprinkle blueberries over top. Cover with the remaining bread cubes.

In a large bowl, whisk eggs, milk, vanilla, and syrup. Drizzle egg mixture evenly over bread. Cover and refrigerate 2 hours or overnight.

Preheat oven to 350 degrees. Cover and bake 30 minutes. Uncover and bake 25–30 minutes more, or until center is firm and top is golden brown. Lightly dust casserole with powdered sugar. Serve with blueberry or maple syrup. Makes 6 servings.

BAKED BREAKFAST BURRITOS

12 **eggs**
³/₄ cup **chunky salsa**
10 **medium flour tortillas**
1 can (4 ounces) **chopped green chiles**
1 cup **grated cheddar cheese**

Preheat oven to 350 degrees.

In a frying pan, scramble eggs and salsa together until firm but not dry. Heat the tortillas in the microwave until softened. Put a spoonful of scrambled egg mixture in the middle of each tortilla. Roll up tortilla and place in a greased 9 x 13-inch pan. Sprinkle with green chiles and cheese. Cover and bake 15 minutes. Makes 6–8 servings.

VARIATION: Cook and crumble spicy sausage into the scrambled eggs for a heartier breakfast.

SCRAMBLED EGG AND HAM PIZZA

I tube (13.8 ounces)	**refrigerated pizza crust dough**
8	**eggs**
2 tablespoons	**milk**
	salt and pepper, to taste
1 1/2 cups	**diced fully cooked ham**
I cup	**grated cheddar cheese**

Preheat oven to 400 degrees.

Spread pizza crust dough along bottom and halfway up the sides of a greased 9 x 13-inch pan. Bake 8 minutes.

In a frying pan, scramble and cook eggs and milk until firm but not dry. Season with salt and pepper. Spread scrambled eggs over hot crust. Place ham and cheese evenly over eggs. Bake 8–12 minutes, or until crust is golden brown and cheese is melted. Makes 6–8 servings.

EGGS FOR EVERYBODY

12 **eggs**
1 cup **milk**
1 cup **grated Monterey Jack cheese,** divided
1 pound **bacon,** cooked and crumbled
1 bunch **green onions,** chopped

Preheat oven to 325 degrees.

In a bowl, beat eggs, milk, and half the cheese. Stir in bacon and onions. Pour mixture into a greased 9 x 13-inch pan. Cover and cook 45–55 minutes, or until eggs are set. Immediately top with remaining cheese and serve. Makes 6 servings.

SAUSAGE-HASH BROWN BREAKFAST BAKE

3 1/2 cups **frozen shredded hash browns**
I pound **sausage,** browned and drained
I cup **grated cheddar cheese**
6 **eggs,** beaten
3/4 cup **milk**
I teaspoon **dry mustard**
1/2 teaspoon **salt**
1/2 teaspoon **black pepper**

Spread hash browns into bottom of a greased 9 x 13-inch pan. Sprinkle cooked sausage and cheese over top.

In a bowl, combine eggs, milk, dry mustard, salt, and pepper. Pour egg mixture evenly over sausage and hash browns. Cover and refrigerate 2 hours or overnight.

Remove from refrigerator 20 minutes before baking and preheat oven to 350 degrees. Cover and bake 30 minutes. Uncover and bake 5–8 minutes more, or until center is set. Makes 6–8 servings.

SOUTHWESTERN EGGS

12 **eggs**

12	**eggs**
$^1/_2$ cup	**milk**
2 cans (4 ounces each)	**chopped green chiles**
$^1/_2$ cup	**chopped red bell pepper**
1 cup	**grated cheddar cheese**
1 cup	**grated Monterey Jack cheese**

Preheat oven to 350 degrees.

In a bowl, beat eggs and milk. Set aside.

In a greased 9 x 13-inch pan, layer chiles, bell pepper, and cheese. Pour egg mixture over top. Cover and bake 30–40 minutes, or until eggs are set in the center. Makes 6 servings.

OMELET BRUNCH

18 **eggs**
1 cup **sour cream**
1 cup **milk**
1 teaspoon **salt**
$^1/_4$ cup **chopped green onions**
1 cup **grated cheddar cheese**

Preheat oven to 325 degrees.

In a large bowl, beat eggs, sour cream, milk, and salt. Fold in green onions. Pour mixture into a greased 9 x 13-inch pan. Bake 45–55 minutes, or until eggs are set. Immediately sprinkle cheese over top and cut into squares before serving. Makes 6–8 servings.

CRESCENT, HASH BROWN AND SAUSAGE BAKE

1 tube (8 ounces)	**refrigerated crescent roll dough**
1 package (10.4 ounces)	**sausage links,** browned, drained, and sliced
1 cup	**frozen shredded hash browns**
1 1/2 cups	**grated cheddar cheese**
5	**eggs**
1/3 cup	**milk**
	salt and pepper, to taste

Preheat oven to 375 degrees.

Unroll crescents and press dough over bottom and up the sides of a 12-inch round pizza pan. (Dough up the sides of the pan should have a small lip so when the egg mixture is added, it stays in the crust.) Sprinkle sausage, hash browns, and cheese over dough.

In a bowl, beat eggs, milk, salt, and pepper with a fork. Pour egg mixture over dough. Bake 30 minutes. Serve wedges with fresh salsa. Makes 4–6 servings.

RAISIN FRENCH TOAST CASSEROLE

1 loaf (24 ounces)	**cinnamon raisin bread,** cubed
6	**eggs,** slightly beaten
3 cups	**milk**
2 teaspoons	**vanilla**
	powdered sugar

Place bread cubes into a greased 9 x 13-inch pan.

In a bowl, whisk eggs, milk, and vanilla. Pour egg mixture evenly over bread. Cover and refrigerate 2 hours or overnight.

Remove from refrigerator 20 minutes before baking and preheat oven to 350 degrees. Bake, uncovered, 45–50 minutes, or until golden brown. Sprinkle powdered sugar over top. Serve with maple syrup. Makes 6 servings.

SPINACH FRITTATA

4	**eggs***
1 1/2 cups	**milk**
1/2 teaspoon	**salt**
1 package (10 ounces)	**frozen spinach,** thawed and drained
3/4 cup	**grated cheddar** or **Swiss cheese**

Preheat oven to 400 degrees.

In a bowl, beat eggs, milk, and salt together. Pour mixture into a greased 8 x 8-inch pan. Spread spinach over egg mixture. Bake 17–22 minutes, or until eggs have set. Sprinkle cheese over top. Makes 2–4 servings.

*Large eggs work best for this recipe.

SWISS SAUSAGE CASSEROLE

10	**slices white bread,** cubed
1 pound	**spicy sausage,** browned and drained
1 can (4 ounces)	**sliced mushrooms,** drained
$^3/_4$ cup	**grated cheddar cheese**
1$^1/_2$ cups	**grated Swiss cheese**
8	**eggs,** beaten
2 cups	**half-and-half**
2 cups	**milk**
1 teaspoon	**salt**
1 teaspoon	**black pepper**

Place bread cubes in a greased 9 x 13-inch pan. Crumble cooked sausage over bread. Evenly lay mushrooms over sausage and sprinkle cheeses over top.

In a large bowl, mix eggs, half-and-half, milk, salt, and pepper. Pour egg mixture evenly over cheese. Cover and refrigerate 2 hours or overnight.

Remove from refrigerator 20 minutes before baking and preheat oven to 350 degrees. Cover and bake 30 minutes. Uncover and bake 15–20 minutes more. Makes 6–8 servings.

VEGETARIAN

ASPARAGUS CASSEROLE

I cup **grated cheddar cheese**
2 cups **crushed saltine crackers**
$^1/_4$ cup **butter** or **margarine,** melted
I can (10.75 ounces) **cream of mushroom soup,** condensed
I can (15 ounces) **asparagus spears,** drained with
liquid reserved
$^1/_2$ cup **sliced almonds**

Preheat oven to 350 degrees.

In a bowl, combine cheese and cracker crumbs. Set aside.

In a separate bowl, mix together butter, soup, and the liquid from the can of asparagus. Layer half the cracker mixture into bottom of an 8 x 8-inch pan. Arrange half the asparagus spears over top. Layer half the sliced almonds and half the soup mixture over asparagus. Layer remaining asparagus spears, almonds, and soup mixture over top. Cover with remaining cracker mixture. Bake 20–25 minutes, or until bubbly and golden brown. Makes 4 servings.

STACKED BLACK BEAN TORTILLA PIE

I can (16 ounces)	**refried beans**
I cup	**salsa,** divided
I teaspoon	**minced garlic**
I tablespoon	**dried cilantro**
I can (15 ounces)	**black beans,** rinsed and drained
I	**medium tomato,** chopped
7	**medium flour tortillas**
2 cups	**grated cheddar cheese**

Preheat oven to 400 degrees.

In a bowl, combine refried beans, $^3/_4$ cup salsa, and garlic.

In a separate bowl, combine remaining salsa, cilantro, black beans, and tomato. Place a tortilla in the bottom of a greased pie pan. Spread a fourth of the refried bean mixture over tortilla within $^1/_2$ inch of edge. Sprinkle $^1/_4$ cup cheese over beans and cover with another tortilla. Spoon a third of the black bean mixture over tortilla. Sprinkle $^1/_4$ cup cheese over black bean mixture and cover with another tortilla. Repeat layers, ending with a final layer of refried bean mixture spread over last tortilla. Sprinkle with $^1/_2$ cup cheese. Cover and bake 35–40 minutes. Serve individual pieces of pie with salsa and sour cream. Makes 4–5 servings.

CHUNKY VEGGIE CASSEROLE

2 cups	**water**
I cup	**uncooked white rice**
I bag (16 ounces)	**frozen broccoli florets**
I bag (16 ounces)	**frozen cauliflower florets**
1/3 cup	**water**
I	**medium onion,** chopped
1/3 cup	**butter** or **margarine**
I jar (16 ounces)	**Cheez Whiz**
I can (10.75 ounces)	**cream of chicken soup,** condensed
2/3 cup	**milk**

In a saucepan, bring 2 cups water and rice to a boil. Reduce heat. Cover and simmer 15 minutes, or until water is absorbed.

In a bowl, heat broccoli and cauliflower with 1/3 cup water in microwave on high heat 8 minutes, or until done. Drain vegetables.

Preheat oven to 350 degrees.

In a frying pan, saute onion in butter. Stir cooked rice into onion. Spread rice mixture into a greased 9 x 13-inch pan. Stir vegetables, cheese sauce, soup, and milk into rice mixture. Bake 30–35 minutes, or until bubbly. Makes 6–8 servings.

MOZZARELLA POTATOES

4 **medium potatoes,** peeled
4 **Roma tomatoes,** sliced
1 **large green bell pepper,** seeded and cut into strips
salt and pepper, to taste
1 teaspoon **Italian seasoning**
2 cups **grated mozzarella cheese**
1 cup **sour cream**

Preheat oven to 400 degrees.

In a stockpot, boil potatoes 25–30 minutes until partially cooked, then thinly slice. Layer half each of the potato slices, tomato slices, and bell pepper strips in a greased 9 x 9-inch pan. Season with salt and pepper. Sprinkle half each of the Italian seasoning and mozzarella cheese over vegetables. Repeat layers with remaining potatoes, tomatoes, and bell pepper. Sprinkle remaining seasoning and cheese over vegetables, then spread sour cream over top. Cover and bake 30–40 minutes, or until bubbly. Makes 4 servings.

CREAMY SPINACH CASSEROLE

2 packages (10 ounces each) **frozen chopped spinach**
1 envelope **onion soup mix**
1 container (16 ounces) **sour cream**
$^3/_4$ cup **grated cheddar cheese**

Preheat oven to 350 degrees.

Cook spinach according to package directions and drain. Place in a greased 1$^1/_2$- to 2-quart baking dish. Stir in onion soup mix and sour cream. Sprinkle cheese over top. Bake 20–25 minutes, or until bubbly. Makes 4–6 servings.

GRANDMA'S YUMMY POTATOES

8 **medium potatoes**
I cup **grated cheddar cheese**
$^1/_4$ cup **butter** or **margarine,** melted
I can (10.75 ounces) **cream of chicken soup,** condensed
$^1/_2$ cup **chopped onion**
I small jar **diced pimientos**
I container (16 ounces) **sour cream**
$^3/_4$ cup **crushed corn flakes** or **potato chips**

Preheat oven to 350 degrees.

Peel and shred potatoes. Boil shredded potatoes in water 10–15 minutes and drain.

Stir cheese, butter, soup, onion, pimientos, and sour cream into potatoes. Spread potato mixture into a greased 9 x 13-inch pan. Bake, uncovered, 45–55 minutes, or until bubbly. Sprinkle corn flakes over potatoes and bake 5 minutes more. Makes 6–8 servings.

VARIATION: For a more traditional potato dish, eliminate the pimientos.

GREEN BEAN CASSEROLE

2 cans (14.5 ounces each)	**French-cut green beans,** drained
1 can (10.75 ounces)	**cream of mushroom soup,** condensed
$2/3$ cup	**milk**
$1/3$ cup	**real bacon bits***
$1/4$ teaspoon	**black pepper**
$1 1/4$ cups	**french-fried onions,** divided

Preheat oven to 350 degrees.

Combine all ingredients except onions in a greased $1 1/2$- to 2-quart baking dish. Stir in $1/2$ cup onions. Bake, uncovered, 30 minutes, or until bubbly. Sprinkle remaining onions over top and bake 5 minutes more. Makes 4–6 servings.

*5–7 slices of bacon, cooked and crumbled, may be substituted.

HOMINY CASSEROLE

1	**medium onion,** chopped
1	**large green bell pepper,** seeded and diced
1/2 cup	**butter** or **margarine**
1 can (15.5 ounces)	**white hominy,** drained
1 can (15.5 ounces)	**yellow hominy,** drained
1 can (12 ounces)	**whole kernel corn,** drained
1 can (4 ounces)	**sliced mushrooms,** drained
1/4 cup	**grated Parmesan cheese**
1 cup	**Cheez Whiz**
1/4 cup	**diced pimiento,** drained

Preheat oven to 350 degrees.

In a frying pan, saute onion and bell pepper in butter until tender. Stir remaining ingredients into onion mixture. Spread into a greased 8 x 8-inch pan. Bake 30–35 minutes, or until bubbly. Makes 4–5 servings.

INDIANA CORN LOVER'S CASSEROLE

2	**eggs,** slightly beaten
I can (14.75 ounces)	**cream style corn**
I can (12 ounces)	**whole kernel corn,** drained
$^3/_4$ cup	**sour cream**
3 tablespoons	**butter** or **margarine,** melted
I $^1/_2$ cups	**grated cheddar cheese**
I	**medium onion,** chopped
I can (4 ounces)	**chopped green chiles,** drained
I package (6.5 ounces)	**corn muffin mix**

Preheat oven to 350 degrees.

In a large bowl, combine eggs, corn, sour cream, butter, cheese, onion, and chiles. Gently fold in corn muffin mix until moistened. Spread mixture into a greased 2-quart baking dish. Bake 60–70 minutes, or until golden brown on top and center is set. Makes 4–6 servings.

MEXICAN PIZZA

I tube (13.8 ounces)	**refrigerated pizza crust dough**
I can (16 ounces)	**refried beans**
$^3/_4$ cup	**chunky salsa**
I envelope	**taco seasoning**
I$^1/_2$ cups	**grated Mexican-blend cheese**
I bag (10 ounces)	**shredded lettuce**
2	**Roma tomatoes,** diced
I$^1/_2$ cups	**crushed nacho cheese tortilla chips**

Preheat oven to 400 degrees.

Cover bottom and partially up the sides of a greased 9 x 13-inch pan with pizza dough. Bake 10–12 minutes, or until light golden brown.

In a saucepan, heat refried beans and salsa together until bubbly. Stir taco seasoning into refried bean mixture. Spread refried bean mixture over baked crust. Sprinkle cheese over beans and bake 5–8 minutes, or until cheese is melted. Layer lettuce, tomatoes, and crushed tortilla chips over top and serve immediately. Makes 5–7 servings.

RICE AND GREEN CHILE CASSEROLE

1 box (6 ounces) **instant long grain and wild rice mix**
1 cup **sour cream**
1 can (4 ounces) **chopped green chiles,** drained
1 cup **grated cheddar cheese**
1 cup **grated Monterey Jack cheese**

Prepare rice according to package directions.

Preheat oven to 350 degrees.

In a bowl, mix together sour cream and green chiles. Spread half the cooked rice over bottom of a greased 8 x 8-inch pan. Spoon half the sour cream mixture over rice. Sprinkle half of each cheese over top. Spoon remaining rice over cheese. Spread remaining sour cream mixture over rice, then sprinkle remaining cheese over top. Bake, uncovered, 15–20 minutes, or until bubbly. Makes 4–6 servings.

SWEET ONION CASSEROLE

6 **large sweet onions,** thinly sliced
6 tablespoons **butter** or **margarine,** divided
1 can (10.75 ounces) **cream of celery soup,** condensed*
$^1/_3$ cup **milk**
$^1/_2$ teaspoon **black pepper**
2 cups **grated Swiss cheese,** divided
6 **slices French bread,** cut 1-inch thick

In a large frying pan, saute onions in 4 tablespoons butter 11−13 minutes, or until onions are tender.

In a large bowl, combine soup, milk, pepper, and 1$^1/_2$ cups cheese.

Preheat oven to 350 degrees. Stir onions into soup mixture. Spread mixture into a greased 9 x 13-inch pan. Sprinkle remaining cheese over top. Melt remaining butter and brush it over one side of each bread slice. Place bread slices, butter side up, in the pan, making three rows. Bake 24−28 minutes. Cool 5−7 minutes before serving. Makes 6 servings.

*Other varieties of condensed cream soups may be substituted.

VEGGIE SHEPHERD'S PIE

1 bag (16 ounces) **frozen California-blend vegetables**
1 can (10.75 ounces) **cheddar cheese soup,** condensed
1/2 teaspoon **thyme**
2 cups **mashed potatoes,** seasoned with garlic*

Preheat oven to 350 degrees.

In a greased 9 x 9-inch pan, combine frozen vegetables, soup, and thyme. Spread potatoes evenly over vegetable layer. Cover and bake 25 minutes. Uncover and bake 15–20 minutes more, or until heated through. Makes 4 servings.

*Instant potatoes may be substituted.

VEGETABLE STUFFING CASSEROLE

1 bag (16 ounces) **frozen green beans**
1 bag (16 ounces) **frozen mixed vegetables**
2 cans (10.75 ounces each) **cream of mushroom soup,** condensed
1 can (6 ounces) **french-fried onions**
1 box (6 ounces) **seasoned stuffing mix**
3 tablespoons **butter** or **margarine,** melted
$^1/_4$ cup **water**

Preheat oven to 350 degrees.

Pour frozen vegetables into bottom of a greased 9 x 13-inch pan. Stir soup into vegetables. Sprinkle onions and stuffing mix evenly over top. Drizzle melted butter and water over stuffing layer. Cover and bake 55–65 minutes, or until heated through. Makes 7–9 servings.

BAKED CHEESY ZUCCHINI

1 medium **zucchini,** thinly sliced
1 **sweet onion,** thinly sliced
2 **Roma tomatoes,** thinly sliced
2 tablespoons **butter** or **margarine,** melted
$^3/_4$ cup **Italian-flavored breadcrumbs**
1 cup **grated mozzarella cheese**

Preheat oven to 350 degrees.

In a greased 9 x 9-inch pan, layer zucchini, onion, and tomatoes. Drizzle butter over vegetables. Sprinkle breadcrumbs over top. Cover and bake 45–50 minutes, or until vegetables are tender. Remove from oven, uncover, and sprinkle cheese over top. Bake 5–7 minutes more, or until cheese is bubbly. Makes 4 servings.

Chicken

BROCCOLI CHICKEN CASSEROLE

2 cups **chopped cooked chicken**
I can (10.75 ounces) **cream of mushroom soup,** condensed
$^1/_4$ cup **milk**
$^3/_4$ cup **grated Monterey Jack cheese**
I package (10 ounces) **frozen broccoli,** thawed
$^1/_2$ cup **green onion,** sliced
$^1/_2$ teaspoon **black pepper**

Preheat oven to 350 degrees.

In a large bowl, mix all ingredients together. Spread mixture into a greased 9 x 13-inch pan. Bake 35–40 minutes, or until bubbly. Makes 4–6 servings.

CASHEW CHICKEN

I package (6.2 ounces)	**fried rice,** with seasoning packet
2 cups	**water**
2	**boneless, skinless chicken breasts,** cooked and cubed
$^1/_2$ cup	**sliced celery**
I can (4 ounces)	**water chestnuts,** drained
$^2/_3$ cup	**cashews**

Preheat oven to 350 degrees.

In a bowl, combine rice, seasoning packet, and water.

Layer chicken, rice mixture, celery, and water chestnuts in a greased 9 x 9-inch pan. Cover and bake 30–40 minutes, or until rice is done. Sprinkle with cashews. Makes 2–4 servings.

CHEESY CHICKEN

4 to 6	**boneless, skinless chicken breasts**
1 carton (16 ounces)	**sour cream**
1 can (10.75 ounces)	**cream of celery soup,** condensed
1 can (10.75 ounces)	**cream of chicken soup,** condensed
1 1/4 cups	**water**
2 cups	**uncooked white rice**
1 cup	**grated cheddar cheese**

Preheat oven to 325 degrees.

Place chicken in a greased 9 x 13-inch pan.

In a bowl, combine sour cream, soups, water, and uncooked rice. Pour over chicken. Cover and bake 1 hour. Sprinkle with cheese immediately before serving. Makes 4–6 servings.

RITZY CHICKEN

4	**boneless, skinless chicken breasts**
I can (10.75 ounces)	**cream of chicken soup,** condensed
I can (10.75 ounces)	**cheddar broccoli soup,** condensed
$^1/_3$ cup	**milk**
$1^1/_2$ cups	**sour cream**
2 cups	**cooked white rice**
25 to 35	**butter-flavor crackers,** crumbled

Preheat oven to 375 degrees.

Place chicken in a greased 9 x 13-inch pan.

In a bowl, combine all remaining ingredients except crackers. Pour over chicken. Bake 45 minutes, or until chicken is done. During last 5–10 minutes of baking, sprinkle cracker crumbs over top. Makes 4 servings.

TORTILLA CHIP ENCHILADAS

2 cups	**chopped cooked chicken**
2 cans (10.75 ounces each)	**cream of chicken soup,** condensed
1 cup	**sour cream**
1/4 cup	**chopped onion**
1 bag (12 ounces)	**tortilla chips,** crushed in bag
1 cup	**grated Monterey Jack cheese**
1/2 cup	**salsa**

Preheat oven to 350 degrees.

In a large bowl combine chicken, soup, sour cream, and onion.

In a greased 9 x 13-inch pan, layer half the chips and half the soup
mixture. Repeat layers. Top with cheese and bake 30 minutes. Serve
with salsa. Makes 6–8 servings.

CORN BREAD CHICKEN CASSEROLE

4 cups **uncooked egg noodles**
3 cups **chopped cooked chicken**
2 cans (10.75 ounces each) **cream of celery soup,** condensed
1 can (15 ounces) **cream style corn**
2 cups **grated cheddar cheese**
1 package **corn bread mix** (8 x 8-inch pan size)

Preheat oven to 350 degrees.

Boil noodles 5–7 minutes, or until cooked. Drain and mix with chicken, soup, corn, and cheese. Pour noodle mixture into a greased 9 x 13-inch pan.

In a bowl, combine corn bread mix with ingredients listed on package. Spoon corn bread batter over noodle mixture. Bake 25–30 minutes, or until corn bread top is golden brown. Makes 6 servings.

FAMILY-FRIENDLY CHICKEN ENCHILADAS

3 cups	**cooked and shredded chicken**
2 cans (10.75 ounces each)	**cream of chicken soup,** condensed
1 cup	**sour cream**
1 can (4 ounces)	**diced green chiles,** drained
$1/4$ cup	**dried minced onion**
$2^1/2$ cups	**grated cheddar cheese,** divided
10	**medium flour tortillas**
$1/3$ cup	**milk**

Preheat oven to 350 degrees.

Combine chicken, 1 can soup, sour cream, chiles, onion, and $1^1/2$ cups cheese. Fill tortillas with $1/3$ to $1/2$ cup chicken mixture. Roll filled tortillas and place seam side down in a greased 9 x 13-inch pan. Combine remaining soup with milk and spread over tortilla rolls. Sprinkle remaining cheese over top. Cover and bake 25 minutes. Uncover and bake 5–10 minutes more, or until heated through. Makes 6–8 servings.

VARIATION: 1 can (10 ounces) enchilada sauce can be used to top enchiladas in place of the soup-and-milk mixture.

FIESTA CHICKEN CASSEROLE

2 cups **uncooked small shell pasta**
2 cups **chopped cooked chicken**
1 jar (16 ounces) **medium salsa**
2 cups **grated Mexican-blend cheese**

Preheat oven to 350 degrees.

Cook pasta according to package directions and drain. Combine all ingredients in a greased 9 x 13-inch pan. Cover and bake 20–25 minutes, or until heated through. Makes 4–6 servings.

CREAMY CHICKEN AND RICE

2 cups **uncooked white rice**
2 cans (10.75 ounces each) **cream of chicken soup,** condensed
2 cups **water**
1 envelope **onion soup mix,** divided
4 to 6 **boneless, skinless chicken breasts**

Preheat oven to 375 degrees.

In a bowl, combine rice, chicken soup, water, and half the onion soup mix. Spread mixture into a greased 9 x 13-inch pan. Lay chicken over top. Sprinkle remaining onion soup mix over chicken. Cover and bake 2 hours. Makes 4–6 servings.

*This casserole can also be baked at 300 degrees for 3 hours.

GRANDMA'S CHICKEN POTPIE

2 cups	**frozen Normandy** or **California-style vegetables**
1 1/2 cups	**cubed cooked chicken**
2 cans (10.75 ounces each)	**cream of chicken soup,** condensed
3/4 cup	**milk**
1/2 teaspoon	**thyme** or **rosemary**
1/2 teaspoon	**black pepper**
1 can (10 ounces)	**refrigerated flaky biscuits**

Preheat oven to 400 degrees.

Cook and cut vegetables into bite-size pieces.

In a greased 3-quart baking dish, combine all ingredients except biscuits. Bake, uncovered, 15 minutes, then remove from oven and stir. Quickly cut biscuits in half. Place biscuit halves, cut side down, over hot chicken and vegetable mixture. Bake 15–20 minutes more, or until biscuits are golden brown and done in the center. Makes 5–7 servings.

GREEN BEAN CHICKEN CASSEROLE

I tablespoon	**olive oil**
4	**boneless, skinless chicken breasts**
3 to 4 cans (14.5 ounces each)	**French-cut green beans,** drained
I can (10.75 ounces)	**cream of mushroom** or **chicken soup,** condensed
$^3/_4$ cup	**mayonnaise**
I teaspoon	**garlic powder**
$^1/_3$ cup	**grated Parmesan cheese**

Preheat oven to 350 degrees.

In a large frying pan, heat olive oil. Lightly brown chicken 3 minutes on each side. Meanwhile, spread green beans evenly in bottom of a greased 9 x 13-inch pan. Lay chicken over green beans.

In a bowl, combine soup, mayonnaise, and garlic powder. Spread soup mixture evenly over chicken and beans. Sprinkle Parmesan over top. Bake, uncovered, 35–40 minutes, or until chicken is done. Makes 4 servings.

HOME-STYLE CHICKEN CASSEROLE

4 cups **frozen shredded hash browns,** thawed
I can (6 ounces) **french-fried onions,** divided
6 slices **processed American cheese**
2 **boneless, skinless chicken breasts,** cubed
I can (10.75 ounces) **cream of chicken soup,** condensed
3/4 cup **milk**
I can (12 ounces) **whole kernel corn,** drained

Preheat oven to 375 degrees.

Stir hash browns and half the onions together. Spread mixture into a greased 9 x 13-inch pan. Lay cheese slices evenly over hash browns. Place chicken cubes evenly over top.

In a bowl, stir together soup and milk. Pour soup mixture over chicken. Bake, uncovered, 30 minutes. Spoon corn over chicken and then stir in the pan. Bake, uncovered, 15 minutes more. Sprinkle remaining onions over top. Bake an additional 5 minutes. Let cool 5–7 minutes before serving. Makes 6 servings.

SWEET LEMONY CHICKEN

6 **boneless, skinless chicken breasts**
2 tablespoons **butter** or **margarine,** melted
$^1/_3$ cup **flour**
$^1/_3$ cup **honey**
$^1/_4$ cup **lemon juice**
1 tablespoon **soy sauce**

Preheat oven to 350 degrees.

Dip chicken in butter and then in flour. Place in a greased 9 x 13-inch pan. Combine honey, lemon juice, and soy sauce. Pour sauce over chicken. Cover and bake 40 minutes, or until chicken is done. Makes 6 servings.

MANGO CHICKEN

1 cup **uncooked white rice**
2 cups **water**
4 **boneless, skinless chicken breasts**
1 jar (12 ounces) **mango salsa**

Preheat oven to 350 degrees.

In a greased 9 x 13-inch pan, combine rice and water. Lay chicken over rice and pour mango salsa over top. Cover and bake 1 hour. Makes 4 servings.

PINEAPPLE CHICKEN

2 cups **diced cooked chicken**
I can (8 ounces) **crushed pineapple,** with liquid
I cup **chopped celery**
I cup **cooked white rice**
I can (10.75 ounces) **cream of mushroom soup,** condensed
I cup **mayonnaise**
I can (6 ounces) **sliced water chestnuts,** drained
2 cups **breadcrumbs**
I tablespoon **butter** or **margarine,** melted

Preheat oven to 350 degrees.

In a large bowl, combine all ingredients except breadcrumbs and butter. Transfer mixture to a greased 9 x 13-inch pan. Combine breadcrumbs and butter; sprinkle over top of chicken mixture. Bake 30–45 minutes. Makes 6–8 servings.

SOUTHWESTERN CHICKEN ROLL-UPS

1 cup	**finely crushed cheese crackers**
1 envelope	**taco seasoning**
4 to 6	**boneless, skinless chicken breasts**
4 to 6	**slices Monterey Jack cheese**
1 can (4 ounces)	**chopped green chiles**

Preheat oven to 350 degrees.

On a plate, combine crackers and taco seasoning. Flatten chicken with a meat tenderizer and place 1 slice cheese and about 1 tablespoon chiles on each piece of chicken. Roll chicken and secure with a toothpick. Sprinkle chicken with cracker mixture and place in a greased 9 x 13-inch pan. Bake, uncovered, 35–40 minutes, or until chicken is done. Remember to remove toothpicks before serving. Makes 4–6 servings.

SWISS CHICKEN

4 to 6 **boneless, skinless chicken breasts**
4 to 6 **slices Swiss cheese**
I can (10.75 ounces) **cream of mushroom soup,** condensed*
$^1/_4$ cup **milk**
I box (6 ounces) **seasoned stuffing mix**
$^1/_4$ cup **butter** or **margarine,** melted

Preheat oven to 350 degrees.

Lay chicken in bottom of a greased 9 x 13-inch pan. Place cheese slices over chicken.

In a bowl, mix together soup and milk. Spoon soup mixture over chicken. Sprinkle dry stuffing mix over soup layer and drizzle butter over top. Cover and bake 55–65 minutes, or until chicken is done. Makes 4–6 servings.

*Cream of chicken soup may be substituted.

TERIYAKI CHICKEN

2	**boneless, skinless chicken breasts,** cubed
I can (15 ounces)	**chicken broth**
2 tablespoons	**brown sugar**
2 tablespoons	**soy sauce**
$^1/_2$ teaspoon	**ground ginger**
$^1/_2$ teaspoon	**Worcestershire sauce**
I cup	**uncooked white rice**
I can (8 ounces)	**pineapple chunks,** drained

Preheat oven to 350 degrees.

Combine all ingredients in a large bowl. Transfer mixture to a greased
9 x 13-inch pan. Cover and bake I hour, or until rice is done. Makes 4
servings.

WILD RICE AND CHICKEN

I package (6.2 ounces)	**long grain and wild rice,** with seasoning packet
1 1/2 cups	**water**
4	**boneless, skinless chicken breasts**
1/2 teaspoon	**dried basil**
1/2 teaspoon	**garlic powder**

Preheat oven to 375 degrees.

In a bowl, combine rice, seasoning packet, and water. Pour mixture into a greased 9 x 13-inch pan. Place chicken over rice mixture and sprinkle with basil and garlic powder. Cover and bake I hour. Makes 4 servings.

DELICIOUS CHICKEN

3 tablespoons **butter** or **margarine,** melted
3 cups **potatoes,** peeled and thinly sliced
1 package (16 ounces) **frozen corn**
2 teaspoons **salt,** divided
2 teaspoons **basil,** divided
1 cup **graham cracker crumbs**
1/3 cup **butter** or **margarine,** melted
4 to 6 **boneless, skinless chicken breasts**

Preheat oven to 375 degrees.

Pour 3 tablespoons melted butter in the bottom of a 9 x 13-inch pan. Combine potatoes and corn in the pan, and then sprinkle with 1 teaspoon salt and 1 teaspoon basil.

In a small bowl, combine cracker crumbs and remaining salt and basil. Transfer mixture to a plate. Dip chicken in 1/3 cup melted butter then roll in crumb mixture, coating completely. Place chicken over vegetables. Cover and bake 60–75 minutes, or until chicken is done and vegetables are tender. Remove from oven, uncover, and bake 10 minutes more to brown chicken. Makes 4–6 servings.

TURKEY

AFTER THANKSGIVING CASSEROLE

1 box (6 ounces) **seasoned stuffing mix**
3 cups **chopped cooked turkey**
2 cups **turkey gravy,** divided
2 cups **mashed potatoes,** seasoned with garlic*

Preheat oven to 350 degrees.

Prepare stuffing according to package directions. Spoon stuffing in a greased 2-quart baking dish. Lay turkey over stuffing. Pour 1 cup gravy over turkey. Spread mashed potatoes evenly over top. Cover with remaining gravy. Cover and bake 35–45 minutes, or until bubbly. Makes 4–6 servings.

*Instant mashed potatoes may be substituted.

VARIATION: Try adding $3/4$ cup frozen peas as a layer between the stuffing and the turkey.

TURKEY TORTILLA CASSEROLE

3 cups	**chopped cooked turkey**
1 can (4 ounces)	**chopped green chiles**
$^3/_4$ cup	**chicken broth**
2 cans (10.75 ounces each)	**cream of chicken soup,** condensed
1	**medium onion,** chopped
8 to 10	**medium gordita-style flour tortillas**
2 cups	**grated Monterey Jack cheese**

Preheat oven to 350 degrees.

In a large bowl, combine turkey, chiles, broth, soup, and onion. Cover bottom of a greased 9 x 13-inch pan with half the tortillas. Spread half the turkey mixture over tortilla layer. Sprinkle half the cheese over top. Repeat layers. Bake 25–30 minutes, or until bubbly and heated through. Makes 6–8 servings.

PAULA'S TURKETTI

1 can (10.75 ounces) **cream of mushroom soup,** condensed
$^1/_2$ cup **water**
2 cups **cubed cooked turkey**
1 $^1/_3$ cups **spaghetti,** broken, cooked, and drained
$^1/_3$ cup **chopped green bell pepper**
$^1/_2$ cup **chopped onion**
$^1/_2$ teaspoon **salt**
$^1/_4$ teaspoon **black pepper**
2 cups **grated cheddar cheese,** divided

Preheat oven to 350 degrees.

In a large bowl, combine soup and water. Stir in remaining ingredients except 1 cup cheese. Spread mixture in a greased 9 x 13-inch pan. Sprinkle remaining cheese over top. Bake 45 minutes. Makes 6–8 servings.

POPPY SEED CASSEROLE

1 1/2 pounds	**ground turkey**
1	**green** or **red bell pepper,** chopped
3 cans (8 ounces each)	**tomato sauce***
1/2 teaspoon	**salt**
1/2 teaspoon	**black pepper**
1 package (8 ounces)	**cream cheese,** cubed
1/2 cup	**sour cream**
1 cup	**cottage cheese**
1 tablespoon	**poppy seeds**
1 bag (12–18 ounces)	**curly noodles,** cooked and drained
1 teaspoon	**Italian seasoning**
1/2 cup	**grated Parmesan cheese**

Preheat oven to 350 degrees.

Brown turkey and bell pepper together until turkey is done. Drain off liquid. Add tomato sauce, salt, and pepper and simmer over low heat.

In a bowl, combine cream cheese, sour cream, cottage cheese, and poppy seeds, and then mix with drained hot noodles. Place noodle mixture into bottom of a greased 9 x 13-inch pan and top with turkey mixture. Cover and bake 30 minutes. Uncover and bake 10 minutes more. Sprinkle Italian seasoning and Parmesan over top. Makes 6 servings.

*For a more saucy dish, add an extra can of tomato sauce.

STUFFING AND TURKEY CASSEROLE

2 cans (10.75 ounces each) **cream of celery soup,** condensed
1 cup **milk**
$^1/_2$ teaspoon **black pepper**
1 bag (16 ounces) **frozen mixed vegetables,**
thawed and drained
2$^1/_2$ cups **cubed cooked turkey**
1 box (6 ounces) **seasoned stuffing mix***

Preheat oven to 400 degrees.

Mix together soup, milk, pepper, vegetables, and turkey. Spread turkey mixture into a greased 9 x 13-inch pan. Prepare stuffing according to package directions. Spoon stuffing evenly over turkey. Bake 25 minutes, or until heated through. Makes 6 servings.

*For a thicker layer of stuffing, use 2 boxes.

TURKEY AND POTATO BAKE

2 cups **cubed cooked turkey**
2 **medium potatoes,** peeled and thinly sliced
1 **medium onion,** sliced
salt and pepper, to taste
1 can (10.75 ounces) **cream of celery soup,** condensed
1/2 cup **skim milk**

Preheat oven to 350 degrees.

In a greased 8 x 8-inch pan, layer turkey, potatoes, and onion. Sprinkle with salt and pepper.

In a bowl, combine soup and milk. Pour over turkey. Cover and bake 1 hour. Makes 4 servings.

TURKEY DIVAN

2 cups	**diced cooked turkey**
1 package (10 ounces)	**frozen broccoli spears,** cooked
1 can (10.75 ounces)	**cream of chicken soup,** condensed
1/2 cup	**mayonnaise**
1/2 teaspoon	**lemon juice**
1/4 teaspoon	**curry powder**
1/2 cup	**grated sharp cheddar cheese**

Preheat oven to 350 degrees.

Layer turkey and broccoli in a greased 9 x 13-inch pan.

In a bowl, combine soup, mayonnaise, lemon juice, and curry powder.
Pour over turkey and sprinkle with cheese. Cover and bake 40 minutes.
Makes 4–6 servings.

TURKEY NOODLE CASSEROLE

1 bag (12 ounces) **egg noodles**
1 can (10.75 ounces) **cream of celery soup,** condensed
1/2 cup **milk**
1 can (5 ounces) **turkey,** drained
2 cups **grated cheddar cheese**
1/2 cup **crushed potato chips**

Preheat oven to 400 degrees.

Cook noodles according to package directions and drain. Stir soup, milk, turkey, and cheese into hot noodles. Spread noodle mixture into a greased 2-quart baking dish. Bake 15 minutes. Top with crushed potato chips and bake 3–5 minutes more. Makes 4–6 servings.

Pork

BAKED RAVIOLI ALFREDO

I bag (25 ounces) **frozen Italian sausage ravioli**
I bag (16 ounces) **frozen broccoli florets**
I jar (16 ounces) **Alfredo sauce**
$3/4$ cup **milk**
$1/4$ cup **seasoned breadcrumbs**

Preheat oven to 350 degrees.

Place frozen ravioli into bottom of a greased 9 x 13-inch pan. Spread broccoli over ravioli. Pour Alfredo sauce over broccoli. Drizzle milk evenly over top. Cover and bake 50 minutes. Uncover and sprinkle breadcrumbs over top. Bake, uncovered, 10 minutes more, or until heated through. Makes 6 servings.

SAUSAGE SPAGHETTI CASSEROLE

I pound	**sausage**
I	**medium onion,** chopped
I jar (26 ounces)	**spaghetti sauce**
$^1/_2$ cup	**water**
I package (16 ounces)	**spaghetti noodles,** cooked and drained
$^1/_4$ cup	**butter** or **margarine,** melted
3	**eggs,** beaten
$^1/_2$ cup	**grated Parmesan cheese**
2 cups	**grated mozzarella cheese,** divided
I container (16 ounces)	**cottage cheese**

Preheat oven to 350 degrees.

In a frying pan, brown sausage and onion together and drain any excess grease. Stir spaghetti sauce and water into sausage mixture. Allow sauce to simmer over low heat 5 minutes.

In a bowl, combine cooked spaghetti, butter, eggs, Parmesan, and half the mozzarella cheese. Spread noodle mixture into a greased 9 x 13-inch pan. Evenly spread cottage cheese over noodles. Spread spaghetti sauce mixture evenly over top. Sprinkle remaining cheese over sauce. Cover and bake 25 minutes. Uncover and bake 10–15 minutes more. Makes 6–8 servings.

CANADIAN BACON PIZZA BAKE

2 tubes (7.5 ounces each) **refrigerated buttermilk biscuits**
1 jar (14 ounces) **pizza sauce**
1 cup **grated Italian-blend cheese**
15 to 20 slices **Canadian bacon**
1 1/2 cups **grated mozzarella cheese,** divided

Preheat oven to 375 degrees.

Separate biscuits and cut each one into 4 pieces. Place in a large bowl and toss with pizza sauce and Italian blend cheese. Place biscuit mixture into a greased 9 x 13-inch pan. Place Canadian bacon slices evenly over top. Sprinkle mozzarella cheese over top. Bake 20–25 minutes, or until biscuits are done. Makes 6 servings.

BROCCOLI AND HAM POTPIE

I package (10 ounces)	**frozen chopped broccoli,** thawed
I can (15 ounces)	**whole kernel corn,** drained
I can (10.75 ounces)	**cream of mushroom soup,** condensed
2 cups	**chopped fully cooked ham**
1 1/2 cups	**grated cheddar cheese**
3/4 cup	**sour cream**
1/2 teaspoon	**black pepper**
I	**refrigerated pie crust**

Preheat oven to 425 degrees.

Spread broccoli into bottom of a lightly greased and microwaveable 10-inch deep-dish pie pan or 1 1/2-quart round dish.

In a bowl, mix corn, soup, ham, cheese, sour cream, and pepper together. Spoon mixture over broccoli. Cover with a paper towel and microwave on high heat 3–4 1/2 minutes, or until hot. Place unfolded pie crust over ham mixture and tuck edges inside pan. Cut four 1-inch slits in crust to allow steam to escape during baking. Place pan on top of a baking sheet. Bake 15 minutes, or until crust turns golden brown. Makes 4–6 servings.

CHEDDAR HAM NOODLE CASSEROLE

I bag (12 ounces)	**egg noodles**
¹/₄ cup	**diced green bell pepper**
¹/₂	**medium onion**
I tablespoon	**olive oil**
I can (10.75 ounces)	**cream of golden mushroom soup,** condensed
²/₃ cup	**milk**
I¹/₂ cups	**diced fully cooked ham**
2 cups	**grated cheddar cheese**

Preheat oven to 400 degrees.

Cook noodles according to package directions and drain.

In a frying pan, saute bell pepper and onion in olive oil until onion is translucent. Stir soup, milk, ham, vegetables, and cheese into warm noodles. Spread noodle mixture into a greased 2-quart baking dish. Bake 15 minutes, or until heated through. Makes 4–6 servings.

CHICAGO-STYLE PIZZA CASSEROLE

2 tubes (13.8 ounces each) **refrigerated pizza crust dough**
2 cups **traditional spaghetti sauce,** divided
1 pound **sausage,** browned and drained
1/2 **medium onion,** chopped
2 cups **grated mozzarella cheese,** divided

Preheat oven to 375 degrees.

Spread 1 crust over bottom and up the sides of a lightly greased 9 x 13-inch pan. Spread 1 1/2 cups sauce over crust. Spread cooked sausage and onion over sauce. Sprinkle 1 1/2 cups cheese over sausage layer. Place remaining pizza crust over top and pinch dough from the lower and upper crusts together. Cut 1-inch slits in top crust. Carefully spread remaining sauce and cheese over top. Bake 30 minutes, or until crust is golden brown and done in the center. Makes 6–8 servings.

COUNTRY BROCCOLI, CHEESE, AND HAM

1 package (10 ounces)	**frozen broccoli**
1 cup	**diced fully cooked ham**
1 can (10.75 ounces)	**cheddar cheese soup,** condensed
1/2 cup	**sour cream**
2 cups	**breadcrumbs**
1 tablespoon	**butter** or **margarine,** melted

Preheat oven to 350 degrees.

Cook broccoli according to package directions. In a large bowl, combine all ingredients except breadcrumbs and butter. Transfer mixture into a greased 9 x 13-inch pan. Combine breadcrumbs and butter, and then sprinkle over mixture. Bake 30–35 minutes. Makes 4–6 servings.

HAM-AND-SWISS PORK CHOPS

6 **pork chops**
1 tablespoon **butter** or **margarine**
12 **fresh bay leaves**
6 **slices ham**
2 tablespoons **chopped fresh sage**
1 cup **grated Swiss cheese**

Preheat oven to 375 degrees.

In a frying pan, brown pork chops in butter 2–3 minutes on each side. Set on a plate lined with paper towels to drain.

In a greased 9 x 13-inch pan, layer pork chops, bay leaves, ham, sage, and cheese. Cover and bake 25 minutes. Makes 4–6 servings.

HASH BROWN HEAVEN

4 cups **frozen shredded hash browns,** thawed
1 pound **bacon,** cooked and crumbled
$^2/_3$ cup **milk**
$^1/_2$ cup **chopped onion**
$^1/_2$ teaspoon **salt**
$^1/_4$ teaspoon **black pepper**
$^1/_8$ teaspoon **garlic powder** (optional)
2 tablespoons **butter** or **margarine,** melted

Preheat oven to 350 degrees.

Combine all ingredients in a large bowl. Transfer to a greased 8 x 8-inch pan. Bake 45 minutes. Makes 6–8 servings.

VARIATION: Make it cheesy by sprinkling 1 cup grated cheddar cheese over casserole immediately after baking.

JAMBALAYA

$1/2$ cup	**butter** or **margarine**
1	**large onion,** chopped
1	**large green bell pepper,** chopped
$1/2$ cup	**diced celery**
1 tablespoon	**minced garlic**
1 pound	**fully cooked smoked sausage links,** cut into $1/2$-inch slices
3 cups	**chicken broth**
2 cups	**uncooked white rice**
1 cup	**chopped tomatoes**
$1/2$ cup	**chopped green onion**
$1 1/2$ tablespoons	**parsley**
1 tablespoon	**Worcestershire sauce**
1 tablespoon	**Tabasco sauce**

Preheat oven to 375 degrees.

In a frying pan, melt butter. Saute onion, bell pepper, celery, and garlic in butter until tender.

In a large bowl, combine sausage, broth, rice, tomatoes, green onion, parsley, Worcestershire sauce, and Tabasco sauce. Stir sauted vegetables into sausage mixture. Spread into a greased 9 x 13-inch pan. Cover and bake 20 minutes. Stir, cover, and bake 20 minutes more. Stir, cover, and bake a final 5–10 minutes, or until rice is done. Makes 6–8 servings.

ORANGE RICE AND PORK CHOPS

6 **pork chops**
salt and pepper, to taste
1 1/3 cups **uncooked white rice**
1 cup **orange juice**
1 can (10.75 ounces) **chicken and rice soup,** condensed

Preheat oven to 350 degrees.

In a frying pan, brown pork chops 2 minutes on each side and season with salt and pepper. Set aside.

In a greased 9 x 13-inch pan, combine rice and orange juice. Place pork chops over rice. Pour soup over top. Cover and bake 45 minutes. Uncover and cook 10 minutes more, or until done. Makes 6 servings.

SAUSAGE PEPPERONI CASSEROLE

1 pound **sausage**
1 **medium onion,** chopped
1 package (3.5 ounces) **sliced pepperoni**
1 jar (14 ounces) **pizza sauce**
1 1/4 cups **grated mozzarella cheese**
1 cup **biscuit mix**
1 cup **milk**
2 **eggs,** lightly beaten

Preheat oven to 400 degrees.

In a frying pan, brown sausage and onion together until sausage is done. Drain any excess grease then stir in pepperoni. Spread meat mixture into a greased 8 x 8-inch pan. Pour sauce evenly over meat. Sprinkle cheese over sauce.

In a separate bowl, mix biscuit mix, milk, and eggs together. Pour batter evenly over meat mixture and sauce. Bake, uncovered, 25 minutes, or until golden brown. Makes 4–6 servings.

BEEF

ROTINI BAKE

12 ounces **uncooked curly rotini** or **small tube pasta**
1 pound **ground beef**
1 jar (26 ounces) **spaghetti sauce**
2 **eggs,** slightly beaten
1 carton (16 ounces) **cottage cheese**
2 cups **grated mozzarella cheese,** divided
$^1/_2$ cup **grated Parmesan cheese**

Preheat oven to 350 degrees.

Cook noodles according to package directions and drain.

In a frying pan, brown and drain beef while noodles cook. Stir spaghetti sauce into beef.

In a large bowl, combine eggs, cottage cheese, 1 cup mozzarella cheese, and Parmesan cheese. Gently fold cooked pasta into cheese mixture. Spread a third of the beef mixture over bottom of a greased 9 x 13-inch pan. Place half the pasta mixture over beef. Layer another third of beef mixture over noodles. Layer remaining noodles over top, followed by remaining beef mixture. Cover and bake 40 minutes. Uncover and sprinkle remaining mozzarella cheese over top. Return to oven and bake 5–10 minutes more, or until cheese is melted. Makes 6–8 servings.

BEEF POTPIE

1 pound **lean beef stew meat,** cooked
1 package (16 ounces) **frozen mixed vegetables,** thawed
1 jar (12 ounces) **mushroom gravy**
$^{1}/_{2}$ teaspoon **thyme**
1 tube (8 ounces) **refrigerated crescent rolls**

Preheat oven to 375 degrees.

Combine all ingredients except rolls in a greased 9 x 13-inch pan. Bake
20 minutes. Remove from oven and place flattened dough over top.
Return to oven and bake 17–19 minutes, or until crust is golden brown.
Makes 6–8 servings.

CORN BREAD ON CHILI

1 **medium onion,** chopped
1 tablespoon **butter** or **margarine**
2 cans (15 ounces each) **chili with meat and beans**
1 can (11 ounces) **Mexican-style corn,** drained
1 cup **grated cheddar cheese**
1 package **corn bread mix** (8 x 8-inch pan size)

Preheat oven to 425 degrees.

In a frying pan, saute onion in butter until onions are tender. Stir in chili and corn. Spread chili mixture into a greased 9 x 13-inch pan. Sprinkle cheese over top.

In a bowl, mix corn bread mix according to package directions. Pour batter evenly over chili mixture. Bake 25 minutes, or until corn bread is golden brown and set in the center. Makes 6–8 servings.

ENCHILADA CASSEROLE

                    1 pound **ground beef,** browned and drained
     1 can (15 ounces) **chili,** any variety
      1 can (8 ounces) **tomato sauce**
     1 can (10 ounces) **enchilada sauce**
     1 bag (10 ounces) **Fritos corn chips,** divided
                1 cup **sour cream**
                1 cup **grated cheddar cheese**

Preheat oven to 350 degrees.

In a large bowl, combine cooked beef, chili, tomato sauce, and enchilada
sauce. Stir in two-thirds of the chips. Spread mixture into a greased
2-quart baking dish. Bake, uncovered, 24–28 minutes, or until heated
through. Spread sour cream over top. Sprinkle cheese over sour cream.
Crush remaining chips and sprinkle over top. Bake 5–8 minutes more,
or until cheese is melted. Makes 6 servings.

CREAM CHEESE ENCHILADAS

1 pound	**ground beef,** browned and drained
1/2 cup	**chopped onion**
2 cans (8 ounces each)	**tomato sauce**
1/4 cup	**water**
1 1/2 teaspoons	**chili powder**
1/2 teaspoon	**black pepper**
1 package (8 ounces)	**cream cheese,** softened
12	**medium flour tortillas**
2 cups	**grated cheddar cheese**
	shredded lettuce
	sour cream

Preheat oven to 375 degrees.

In a large bowl, combine cooked beef, onion, tomato sauce, water, and spices. Spread cream cheese over tortillas, roll up, and place in a greased 9 x 13-inch pan. Pour beef mixture over tortillas. Sprinkle with cheddar cheese. Cover and bake 25 minutes. Serve over shredded lettuce and top with a dollop of sour cream. Makes 6–8 servings.

CHILIGHETTI

I pound **ground beef,** browned and drained
I package (8 ounces) **spaghetti,** cooked and drained
$^{1}/_{2}$ cup **chopped onion**
I cup **sour cream**
2 cans (8 ounces each) **tomato sauce**
I can (4 ounces) **sliced mushrooms**
2 cans (16 ounces each) **chili,** any type
I clove **garlic,** minced
2 cups **grated cheddar cheese**

Preheat oven to 350 degrees.

In a large bowl, combine all ingredients except cheese. Transfer mixture into a greased 9 x 13-inch pan. Top with cheese. Bake 20 minutes. Makes 6–8 servings.

DEEP-DISH TACOS

$^1/_2$ cup **sour cream**
$^1/_2$ cup **mayonnaise**
$^1/_2$ cup **grated cheddar cheese**
$^1/_4$ cup **chopped onion**
I cup **biscuit mix**
$^1/_4$ cup **cold water**
$^1/_2$ pound **ground beef,** browned and drained
I medium **tomato,** thinly sliced
$^1/_2$ cup **green bell pepper,** chopped

Preheat oven to 375 degrees.

In a bowl, combine sour cream, mayonnaise, cheese, and onion. Set aside.

In a separate bowl, mix biscuit mix and water until a soft dough forms. Press dough on bottom and up the sides of a greased 8 x 8-inch pan. Layer beef, tomato, and bell pepper over dough. Spoon sour cream mixture over top. Bake 25–30 minutes. Makes 4 servings.

COWBOY CASSEROLE

I pound	**ground beef**
I	**medium onion,** chopped
2	**jalapeño peppers,** seeded and diced
2 packages (6.5 ounces each)	**corn bread mix**
$^1/_2$ teaspoon	**salt**
$^1/_2$ teaspoon	**baking soda**
I can (14.75 ounces)	**cream style corn**
$^3/_4$ cup	**milk**
2	**eggs,** beaten
2 cups	**grated cheddar cheese,** divided

Preheat oven to 350 degrees.

In a frying pan, brown beef with onion and peppers until beef is done. Drain any excess grease and set aside.

In a bowl, combine corn bread mix, salt, baking soda, corn, milk, and eggs. Spread half the batter over bottom of a greased 9 x 13-inch pan. Sprinkle half the cheese over batter. Spoon meat mixture evenly over top. Sprinkle remaining cheese over meat mixture, and then spread remaining batter over top. Bake, uncovered, 35 minutes, or until corn bread is golden brown and set in the center. Makes 6–8 servings.

INCREDIBLE CHEESEBURGER PIE

I pound **ground beef,** browned and drained
I cup **chopped onion**
I cup **grated cheddar cheese**
I cup **milk**
$^1/_2$ cup **biscuit mix**
2 **eggs**

Preheat oven to 325 degrees.

In a greased 9 x 9-inch pan, layer beef, onion, and cheese.

In a bowl, combine milk, biscuit mix, and eggs. Spread dough mixture over cheese. Bake 25–35 minutes, or until knife inserted in the center comes out clean. Makes 4 servings.

ITALIAN MACARONI BAKE

8 ounces	**uncooked elbow macaroni**
1 pound	**ground beef,** browned and drained
	salt and pepper, to taste
1 jar (14 ounces)	**pizza sauce**
1 can (4 ounces)	**sliced mushrooms**
2 cups	**grated mozzarella cheese**

Preheat oven to 350 degrees.

Cook macaroni according to package directions and drain.

Season cooked beef with salt and pepper. Place half the macaroni into bottom of a greased 2-quart baking dish. Layer half each of the beef, pizza sauce, mushrooms, and cheese. Place remaining macaroni over top and repeat layers. Cover and bake 20 minutes. Uncover and bake 5–10 minutes more, or until cheese is melted. Makes 6 servings.

MEAT AND POTATO CASSEROLE

I pound	**ground beef**
2	**medium onions,** chopped
I ¹/₂ teaspoons	**Italian seasoning**
4 to 6	**medium potatoes,** peeled and thinly sliced
	salt and pepper, to taste
I can (10.75 ounces)	**cream of mushroom soup,** condensed
¹/₃ cup	**water**

Preheat oven to 350 degrees.

In a frying pan, brown beef and onion together until beef is done. Stir Italian seasoning into beef mixture. Lay a third of the potatoes on bottom of a greased 9 x 13-inch pan. Sprinkle potatoes with salt and pepper. Spread half the beef mixture over top. Repeat layers, ending with potato layer. Combine soup and water. Spread soup mixture over top. Cover and bake I hour. Makes 6–8 servings.

MEATBALL CASSEROLE

I can (10.75 ounces) **cream of chicken soup,** condensed
I cup **sour cream**
I cup **grated cheddar cheese**
I **large onion,** chopped
I teaspoon **salt**
I teaspoon **black pepper**
I package (30 ounces) **frozen shredded hash browns,** thawed
20 **precooked frozen meatballs**

Preheat oven to 350 degrees.

In a bowl, stir together soup, sour cream, cheese, onion, salt, and
pepper. With a paper towel, pat hash browns dry and then stir into
soup mixture. Spread hash brown mixture into a greased 9 x 13-inch
pan. Slightly press meatballs into hash brown mixture in even rows.
Cover and bake 35 minutes. Uncover and bake 10–15 minutes more,
or until hash browns are done. Makes 6–8 servings.

ONION RING BARBECUE BAKE

1 1/2 pounds **ground beef**
1 **medium onion,** chopped
1 jar (18 ounces) **hickory barbecue sauce**
1 bag (16 ounces) **frozen onion rings**

Preheat oven to 425 degrees.

In a frying pan, brown beef and onion together until beef is done. Drain any excess grease. Stir barbecue sauce into beef and onion. Spread beef mixture into a greased 9 x 13-inch pan. Place onion rings evenly over top. Bake 20–25 minutes, or until onion rings are crisp. Makes 6–8 servings.

PIZZA PUFFS

I pound	**ground beef,** browned and drained
I can (15 ounces)	**pizza sauce**
2 tubes (7.5 ounces each)	**refrigerated biscuits**
2 cups	**grated mozzarella cheese**
$^1/_2$ cup	**grated cheddar cheese**

Preheat oven to 400 degrees.

In a bowl, combine cooked beef and pizza sauce. Cut biscuits into
4 pieces each and place in a greased 9 x 13-inch pan. Pour beef mixture
over top. Bake, uncovered, 20–25 minutes. Sprinkle cheese over top.
Bake 3–7 minutes more, or until cheese is melted. Makes 6–8 servings.

SLOPPY JOE PIE

1 pound	**ground beef**
1	**medium onion,** chopped
1 can (15 ounces)	**crushed tomatoes,** with liquid
1 envelope	**sloppy joe seasoning**
1 tube (8 ounces)	**refrigerated crescent roll dough**

Preheat oven to 375 degrees.

In a frying pan, brown beef and onion together until beef is done. Stir crushed tomatoes and seasoning into beef and onion. Simmer over medium-low heat 5 minutes, stirring occasionally. Place beef mixture into a greased, deep 9-inch pie pan or round baking dish. Lay individually flattened crescents over top, placing the skinny point in the center, stretching the bottom edge of the crescent dough triangle to the outside of the pan. Overlap dough if necessary. Bake 15 minutes, or until crust is golden brown. Makes 4–6 servings.

SOUTHWEST CASSEROLE

I pound **ground beef,** browned and drained
2 cans (8 ounces each) **tomato sauce**
I can (12–15 ounces) **whole kernel corn,** drained
I envelope **taco seasoning**
10 **medium gordita-style flour tortillas**
I can (10.75 ounces) **cream of celery soup,** condensed
$^3/_4$ cup **milk**
I $^1/_2$ cups **grated cheddar or
Mexican-blend cheese**

Preheat oven to 350 degrees.

In a bowl, combine cooked beef, tomato sauce, corn, and taco season-ing. Use 6 tortillas to cover bottom and sides of a greased 9 x 13-inch pan. Spread beef mixture over tortillas. Use remaining tortillas to cover beef mixture, cutting to fit if necessary. Mix together soup and milk and pour over tortillas. Sprinkle cheese over top. Bake 20–25 minutes, or until edges turn golden brown. Makes 6–8 servings.

TATER TOT CASSEROLE

1 pound	**ground beef**
1	**medium onion,** chopped
2 cans (10.75 ounces each)	**cream of mushroom** or **cream of chicken soup,** condensed
1 can (14.5 ounces)	**whole kernel corn,** drained
1 cup	**grated cheddar cheese**
1 package (27–32 ounces)	**frozen tater tots**

Preheat oven to 350 degrees.

In a frying pan, brown beef and onion together until beef is done. Drain any excess grease. Place beef mixture into bottom of a greased 9 x 13-inch pan. Spoon 1 can soup over top. Sprinkle corn and cheese over soup layer. Cover with tater tots (lay tater tots on their sides). Spread remaining can of soup over tater tots. Bake 40 minutes. Makes 6–8 servings.

FAMILY
FAVORITES

BAKED MOSTACCIOLI

I pound **ground beef,** cooked and drained
1 1/2 jars (26 ounces each) **spaghetti sauce**
I package (12 ounces) **mostaccioli noodles**
2 cups **grated mozzarella cheese**
1/3 cup **grated Parmesan cheese**

Preheat oven to 350 degrees. Combine beef and spaghetti sauce. Set aside.

Cook noodles according to package directions and drain. In a greased 9 x 13-inch pan, layer half each of the pasta, beef mixture, and mozzarella cheese. Repeat layers, and then top with Parmesan. Cover and bake 40 minutes. Uncover and cook 10 minutes more. Makes 6–8 servings.

FISH AND CHEESY PASTA CASSEROLE

16 ounces **curly pasta,** cooked and drained
1 jar (16 ounces) **Ragu double-cheddar sauce**
5 **frozen battered fish fillets**

Preheat oven to 375 degrees.

Cook pasta according to package directions and drain. Place pasta into a greased 9 x 13-inch pan. Stir cheddar sauce into noodles. Place fish over top. Bake, uncovered, 30 minutes. Makes 5 servings.

BURIED PEPPERONI SUPREME PIZZA

2 tubes (13.8 ounces) **refrigerated pizza crust dough**
2 cans (8 ounces each) **tomato sauce,** divided
1 teaspoon **Italian seasoning**
24 **pepperoni slices**
1 can (4 ounces) **mushroom pieces,** drained
1 can (3.8 ounces) **sliced olives,** drained
2 cups **grated mozzarella cheese,** divided

Preheat oven to 375 degrees.

Spread 1 crust over bottom and up the sides of a lightly greased 9 x 13-inch pan. Spread 1 1/2 cans tomato sauce over bottom crust. Sprinkle Italian seasoning over sauce, and then layer pepperoni, mushrooms, and olives over top. Sprinkle 1 1/2 cups cheese over pepperoni layer. Place remaining pizza crust over top. Pinch the lower and upper dough crust together. Cut four 1-inch slits in top of crust. Spread remaining sauce and cheese over top. Bake 30 minutes, or until crust is golden brown and done in the center. Makes 6–8 servings.

DEEP DISH SAUSAGE PIZZA

1 tube (13.8 ounces) **refrigerated pizza crust dough**
1 can (8 ounces) **tomato sauce**
1 1/2 teaspoons **Italian seasoning**
1 pound **sausage,** browned and drained
1 can (3.8 ounces) **sliced olives,** drained
1/2 **onion,** thinly sliced
1/3 cup **chopped green bell pepper**
1 1/2 cups **grated mozzarella cheese**

Preheat oven to 425 degrees.

Press dough over bottom and halfway up the sides of a lightly greased
9 x 13-inch pan. Bake 9 minutes. Spread sauce over crust. Sprinkle
Italian seasoning and cooked sausage over sauce. Layer olives, onion
and bell pepper over sausage and then sprinkle cheese over top. Bake
7–11 minutes, or until cheese is melted and crust is golden brown.
Makes 6–8 servings.

EASY LASAGNA

1 **egg,** beaten
$^1/_4$ cup **grated Parmesan cheese**
1$^1/_2$ teaspoons **Italian seasoning**
1 container (16 ounces) **cottage cheese,** divided
2 cups **grated mozzarella cheese,** divided
1 pound **ground beef**
1 **medium onion,** chopped
$^1/_2$ cup **water**
2 cans (26 ounces each) **chunky spaghetti sauce**
1 box (12 ounces) **oven-ready lasagna noodles,**
uncooked

Preheat oven to 350 degrees.

In a bowl, combine egg, Parmesan, Italian seasoning, cottage cheese, and 1 cup mozzarella cheese. Set aside.

In a large frying pan, brown beef and onion together until beef is done. Drain any excess grease. Add water and all but 1 cup of spaghetti sauce to beef. Spread reserved spaghetti sauce into bottom of a greased 9 x 13-inch pan. Layer 5 to 6 lasagna noodles over sauce, overlapping or breaking to fit, if necessary. Spread half the cheese mixture over noodles. Spoon a third of the beef mixture over cheese layer. Repeat layers once. Add one more layer of 5 to 6 noodles and spoon remaining third of beef mixture over top. Cover and bake 50 minutes. Sprinkle remaining mozzarella cheese over top. Let stand 5 minutes before serving. Makes 8 servings.

CHILEAN CORN CASSEROLE

4 cans (15 ounces each)	**whole kernel corn,** drained
1 1/2 teaspoons	**basil**
1 teaspoon	**salt**
3 tablespoons	**butter** or **margarine**
1 tablespoon	**cornstarch**
1 1/2 pounds	**ground beef**
3	**large onions,** chopped
1 teaspoon	**ground cumin**
1 can (2.25 ounces)	**sliced black olives,** drained
1/2 cup	**raisins**
2 tablespoons	**sugar**

Preheat oven to 400 degrees.

In a blender, grind corn for 3 minutes. Pour liquefied corn into a saucepan with basil, salt, and butter. Heat until it starts to bubble. Slowly stir in cornstarch to thicken.

In a frying pan, brown beef and onions together. Drain any excess grease. Stir cumin into beef mixture. Spoon beef mixture into bottom of a greased 9 x 13-inch pan. Sprinkle olives and raisins over beef mixture. Spread corn mixture evenly over top. Sprinkle sugar over corn layer. Bake 40–50 minutes, or until golden brown. Makes 6–8 servings.

*This traditional Chilean dish, called *pastel de choclo,* is often served with sugar on the side so sugar can be added to your own liking while eating.

HOME-STYLE SHELLS AND CHEESE

1 package (16 ounces) **small shell pasta**
1 can (10.75 ounces) **tomato soup,** condensed
1 ¹/₂ cups **grated cheddar cheese,** divided

Preheat oven to 350 degrees.

Cook shells according to package directions and drain. Stir soup and
1 cup cheddar cheese into shells. Spread mixture into a greased
9 x 13-inch pan. Sprinkle remaining cheese over top. Bake 25–30
minutes. Makes 6 servings.

MAC AND CHEESE BAKE

3 cups **uncooked elbow macaroni**
1 jar (16 ounces) **Ragu double-cheddar sauce**
1 **green onion,** chopped (optional)
$^1/_4$ cup **seasoned breadcrumbs**

Preheat oven to 400 degrees.

Cook macaroni according to package directions and drain. Stir in cheddar
sauce and onion, if desired. Spread macaroni mixture into a greased
2-quart baking dish. Sprinkle breadcrumbs over top. Cover and bake
12–15 minutes. Uncover and bake 5 minutes more. Makes 4–6 servings.

CHEESEBURGER CASSEROLE

2 pounds	**ground beef**
1	**large onion,** chopped
1 teaspoon	**salt**
$^1/_2$ teaspoon	**black pepper**
$1^3/_4$ cups	**grated cheddar cheese**
1 cup	**biscuit mix**
$1^3/_4$ cups	**milk**
3	**eggs,** lightly beaten

Preheat oven to 400 degrees.

Brown beef and onion together in a large frying pan. Drain any excess grease. Stir salt and pepper into beef and onion. Spread mixture into a greased 9 x 13-inch pan. Sprinkle cheese over top.

In a bowl, mix together biscuit mix, milk, and eggs. Pour batter over top. Bake 25–30 minutes, or until lightly golden brown and set in the center. Makes 6–8 servings.

CHICKEN RICE

1	**green bell pepper,** chopped
1	**medium onion,** chopped
1 cup	**uncooked white rice**
$^1/_2$ cup	**butter** or **margarine**
2 cans (10.75 ounces each)	**chicken and rice soup,** condensed
1 cup	**water**

Preheat oven to 350 degrees.

In a frying pan, saute bell pepper, onion, and rice in butter about 5 minutes.

In a greased 9 x 13-inch pan, combine rice mixture, soup, and water. Cover and bake 45–55 minutes. Makes 6–8 servings.

BAKED BEANS 'N' DOGS

3 cans (15.5 ounces each) **pork and beans**
1 package (8–10 count) **hot dogs,** sliced
$^1/_2$ cup **brown sugar**
$^1/_4$ cup **ketchup**
$^1/_4$ cup **dried minced onion**
2 teaspoons **mustard**

Preheat oven to 350 degrees.

Mix all ingredients together in a 2- to 3-quart baking dish. Bake, uncovered, 45 minutes, or until bubbly. Makes 6–8 servings.

QUICK MEXICAN DINNER

1 pound **ground beef,** browned and drained
1 can (15.5 ounces) **sloppy joe sauce**
1 can (11 ounces) **Mexican-style corn**
2 cups **grated cheddar cheese**
1 tube (6 ounces) **refrigerated biscuits**

Preheat oven to 375 degrees.

Combine cooked beef, sloppy joe sauce, and corn.

Layer beef mixture in the bottom of a 9 x 9-inch pan. Sprinkle cheese over top. Cut biscuits in half and lay over cheese, cut side down. Bake 15–20 minutes. Makes 4–6 servings.

TACO PIE

I tube (8 ounces) **refrigerated crescent roll dough**
I 1/2 pounds **ground beef**
I **medium onion,** chopped
I envelope **taco seasoning**
I cup **salsa**
I 1/2 cups **grated Mexican-blend cheese**
I bag (10 ounces) **shredded lettuce**
2 **Roma tomatoes,** diced
2 cups **crushed nacho cheese tortilla chips**

Preheat oven to 350 degrees.

Cover bottom of a greased 9 x 13-inch pan with crescent dough. Bake 10–14 minutes, or until light golden brown.

In a frying pan, brown beef and onion together until beef is done. Drain any excess grease. Stir taco seasoning and salsa into beef. Spread beef mixture over baked crust. Sprinkle cheese over top. Bake 2–5 minutes, or until cheese is melted. Layer lettuce, tomatoes, and crushed chips over top. Serve immediately. Makes 6 servings.

STUFFED PASTA SHELLS

1 package (12 ounces) **large pasta shells**
1 container (16 ounces) **cottage cheese**
1 **egg,** slightly beaten
2 cups **grated mozzarella cheese**
1 jar (26 ounces) **spaghetti sauce**

Preheat oven to 350 degrees.

Cook shells according to package directions and drain.

In a bowl, combine cottage cheese, egg, and mozzarella. Stuff cooked shells with cheese mixture. Place shells in a lightly greased 9 x 13-inch pan. Pour sauce over shells. Cover and bake 45 minutes, or until sauce is bubbly. Makes 6 servings.

CHILI CASSEROLE

1 bag (14 ounces) **tortilla chips,** crushed
2 cans (15 ounces each) **chili con carne**
1 can (8 ounces) **tomato sauce**
2 cups **grated cheddar cheese**

Preheat oven to 350 degrees.

Sprinkle half the chips over bottom of a glass 9 x 13-inch pan. Spread 1 can chili over chip layer. Drizzle half the tomato sauce over top. Sprinkle 1 cup cheese over sauce. Repeat layers. Bake 17–22 minutes. Serve with salsa on the side. Makes 6 servings.

TUNA-TATER TOT CASSEROLE

1 package (32 ounces) **frozen tater tots**
1 can (6 ounces) **tuna,** drained*
1 can (10.75 ounces) **cream of chicken soup,** condensed
1/2 cup **milk**
1 1/2 cups **grated cheddar cheese**

Preheat oven to 350 degrees.

Place tater tots in a greased 2-quart baking dish. Combine tuna, soup, and milk. Pour over tater tots and then sprinkle with cheese. Cover and bake 1 hour. Makes 6 servings.

*Canned chicken or ham may be substituted.

TRADITIONAL TUNA CASSEROLE

1 bag (12 ounces)	**egg noodles**
1 can (10.75 ounces)	**cream of mushroom soup,** condensed
1/2 cup	**milk**
1 can (6 ounces)	**tuna,** drained
2 cups	**grated cheddar cheese**
1/2 cup	**crushed cheddar and sour cream potato chips**

Preheat oven to 400 degrees.

Cook noodles according to package directions and drain. Stir soup, milk, tuna, and cheese into noodles. Spread noodle mixture into a greased 2-quart baking dish. Bake 15 minutes. Top with crushed chips and bake 3–5 minutes more. Makes 4–6 servings.

VARIATION: Add 1 cup cooked peas to the noodle mixture before baking.

NOTES

NOTES

NOTES

NOTES

ABOUT THE AUTHORS

Stephanie Ashcraft was raised near Kirklin, Indiana. She received a bachelor's degree in family science and a teaching certificate from Brigham Young University. Stephanie loves teaching, interacting with people, and spending time with friends and family. Since 1998, she has taught cooking classes wherever she has lived. Being a mom is her full-time job. For more information about Stephanie and her cooking classes, visit www.recipes-101.com.

Janet Eyring was raised in Utah. She received a bachelor's degree from Brigham Young University. Janet loves spending time with friends and family and teaching classes locally. She and her husband, Sean, reside in Pleasant Grove, Utah, with their children.